MARK THURMAN / EMILY HEARN

Get GRAPHIC!

Using storyboards to write and draw
picture books, graphic novels,
or comic strips

Pembroke Publishers Limited

Pembroke Publishers
538 Hood Road
Markham, Ontario, Canada L3R 3K9
www.pembrokepublishers.com

Distributed in the U.S. by Stenhouse Publishers
480 Congress Street
Portland, ME 04101
www.stenhouse.com

© 2010 Mark Thurman and Emily Hearn

We acknowledge the financial support of the Government of Canada
through the Book Publishing Industry Development Program
(BPIDP) for our publishing activities.

We acknowledge the assistance of the Government of Ontario
through the Ontario Media Development Corporation's Ontario
Book Initiative.

Library and Archives Canada Cataloguing in Publication

Thurman, Mark, 1948-
   Get graphic! : using storyboards to write and draw picture books,
graphic novels,
or comic strips / Mark Thurman, Emily Hearn.

Includes index.
ISBN 978-1-55138-252-4

1. Creative writing (Elementary education). 2. Creative writing
(Secondary education). 3. English language—Composition and
exercises—Study and teaching (Elementary). 4. English language—
Composition and exercises—Study and teaching (Secondary).
5. Storyboards. 6. Pictures in education. I. Hearn, Emily II. Title.

LB1576.T535 2010   371.33'5   C2009-907090-1

Editor: Kat Mototsune
Cover and Design: John Zehethofer

Printed and bound in Canada
9 8 7 6 5 4 3 2 1

Acknowledgments

Many thanks to Claire Fyfe, librarian at multicultural Riverdale Public
Library in Toronto, for the list of children's favorite books. — E.H.

A special thanks to Emily Hearn for teaching me "the ropes" of
dynamic storytelling over the 16 years we created the Mighty Mites
comics. Thanks also to Mary Macchiusi, John Zehethofer, and Kat
Mototsune for being part of the storyboard team. — M.T.

CONTENTS

INTRODUCTION

Storyboarding isn't the way books are written. Our adaptation of the animator's "map" is an educational tool, pure and simple. It works at its richest with kids nurtured on storytelling and process writing. Already in love with words, they enjoy discrimination in their use.

Based on our experience in numerous elementary and secondary school classrooms, *Get Graphic!* introduces the power of a storyboard in all stages of the creative process — from brainstorming ideas, to using thumbnail sketches to develop, revise, and finalize stories. It offers critical information that will direct students to thoughtful writing and exciting illustrations. It will also encourage them to consider design as an essential feature of original picture books, graphic novels, or comic books.

A powerful technique for encouraging students to show action that peaks and resolves, storyboards free young writers to focus on language and build skills connected to highly visual media where words, few but apt, must resonate. Focusing on the visual helps students appreciate how pictures affect the viewer emotionally. It makes students more aware of how TV, computer games, and all forms of media strive to influence them with words and visuals.

Get Graphic! builds on student fascination with new media. It describes good principles of design and encourages students to create and place characters in action that propels the plot along. Step-by-step instructions lead students to generate action-filled pages and streamlined plots for their own unique and personalized stories and books.

We want students to share our fun with story and design and color. We know they enjoy drawing and writing their own picture books, graphic novels, and comic strips, because we have cabinets bulging with photocopies, none of them substitutes for the colored, textured, subtle, poetic works that the young authors invariably want to keep. We don't ask for and haven't been offered a single one. Unspoken thanks.

Plenty of work lies ahead for student and teacher alike, and we wish you the same marvelous enjoyment that storyboarding projects have given us.

Eight Stages to a Book

A storyboard is what you see on pages 88–92. It is a series of white panels divided by black lines, each numbered panel representing a page of the planned book. In other words, a writer's and illustrator's storyboard is a kind of map or miniature plan of a book.

Eight stages carry the author/illustrator from stimulus to the moment when photo and biography are pasted on the inside or outside of the back cover of the completed book. Done!

Some stages are deliberately rapid; others, as time-consuming as the writer/illustrator wishes. The eight stages correspond with the chapters in this book:

Stage 1: Read, Read, Read—reading picture books and graphic novels as stimulus

Stage 2: Invent Your Plot—writing the story

Stage 3: Drawing by Drawing—planning drawings

Stage 4: Storyboarding—using a storyboard to lay out the plot (fast pencil)

Stage 5: Book Mock-Up—making a page-by-page rough copy (fast pencil)

Stage 6: A Full-Color Book—editing the story, color, details, lettering

Stage 7: Using Collage Illustration for a Picture Book—cut-and-paste, collage illustrations

Stage 8: It's a Book!—cover, laminating, binding, sharing

Read, Read, Read

When you want to make a picture book,
graphic novel, or comic strip, here's one way
to go about it. Begin by reading and looking
at lots of books. Some you'll like better than
others because everyone chooses differently.
And isn't that a good thing? Variety means
there is a place for your own story.

Here are some picture books that other kids and librarians have found to be favorites:

Alligator Pie and others by Dennis Lee; illustrated by Frank Newfeld and others.

The Basketball Player and others by Roch Carrier.

Boo Hoo Bird by Jeremy Tankard.

Class Clown and others by Robert Munsch; illustrated by Michael Martchenko and others.

Click, Clack, Moo: Cows That Type by Dorren Cronin; illustrated by Betty Lewin.

The Day Leo Said I Hate You by Robie Harris; illustrated by Molly Bang.

Don't Let the Pigeon Drive the Bus by Mo Willems.

Franklin Says I Love You and others; by Paulette Bourgeois; illustrated by Brenda Clark.

I'd Really Like to Eat a Child by Sylviane Donnio; illustrated by Dorothee De Monfreid.

I've Walked Alone and others by Barbara Reid.

Jillian Jiggs and the Great Big Snow and others by Phoebe Gilman.

Monkey Business by Wallace Edwards.

Prehistoric Pinkerton by Stephen Kellog.

Scaredy Squirrel by Melanie Watt.

Stella Star of the Sea; Stella Queen of the Snow by Marie-Louise Gay.

Stellaluna by Jannell Cannon.

Zen Shorts by Jon Mukin.

These are popular graphic novels/comic strips and series:

Babymouse Queen of the World by Jennifer and Matthew Holme.

Chiggers by Hope Larson.

John Fuller, the Fog Mound series by Susan Schade.

Johnny Boo: The Best Little Ghost in the World by James Kochalka.

Sardine in Outer Space, the Space Pirates series by Emmanuel Guibert; illustrated by Joann Sfar.

Silly Lily and the Four Seasons: a toon book by Agnes Rosenstiehl.

Classic Series

Asterix series by Rene Goscinny; ill. by Albert Uderzo

Tintin series by Hergé

Other Series

The Baby-Sitters Club Graphix series by Ann M. Martin and Raina Telgemeier.

Bone series by Jeff Smith.

Captain Underpants series by Dav Pilkey.

Little Vampire series by Joann Sfar.

More on Reading

• Read and read and read to your children. Choose your own favorites because your enjoyment will be contagious and the publishing market continues to offer new delights.

• Use well-illustrated picture books that are proven favorites with young children to reinforce the concepts you will find in this book. Begin with the classics:

Brown, Margaret Wise; ill. by Clement Hurd. *The Runaway Bunny.*
Gentle, whimsical, magical; two pages of text with black-and-white illustrations alternate with full-color double-page spreads.

Dr. Seuss, any in the series; a couple of examples:
The 500 Hats of Bartholomew Cubbins.
A classic; an offbeat masterpiece; black-and-white illustrations; color red used for the hat only—must be an important hat?; variety of viewpoints; cartoon style.

Scrambled Eggs Super!
A nonstop series of viewpoints and crazy characters; black-line brush drawings; the colors red, blue, and yellow create dynamic and unusual effects; visual repetition of two eggs/two birds.

Keats, Ezra Jack. *The Snowy Day.*
Full-color, mutimedia collage illustrations; masterful use of bold color, texture, and white space; rhythmic, elegant page design. See also *John Henry, an American Legend* and *Whistle for Willie.*

McKlosky, Robert. *Blueberries for Sal.*
Single-color, dark blue-black illustrations; variety of dynamic viewpoints; illustrations have the expansive and dynamic quality of the outdoors.

Sendak, Maurice. *Where the Wild Things Are.*
A classic in all respsects; gentle yet dynamic, wild and crazy full-color illustrations; minimal text; the story starts with a small frame, centre page, that grows until it covers three double-page spreads where the wild rumpus occurs; illustrations get smaller as the plot goes back to reality; at wake-up time, supper is still hot (no picture).

Van Allsburg, Chris. *The Polar Express.*
Exquisite, full-color, textured, chalk pastel drawings; marvelous viewpoints; traditional text/illustrations, page format; all double-page spreads bordered with a black ink outline. See also *Jumanji; The Garden of Abdul Gasazi; Ben's Dream;* and *The Mysteries of Harris Burdick.*

Wildsmith, Brian. *The Circus.*
Bold, dynamic, highly textured, full-color, multimedia collage illustrations. See also *Wild Animals.*

8

The way we use picture books in workshops may help you adapt your selection to feature the significant concepts. Here are a couple of examples:

• Books like *The Great Big Fire Engine Book* by Tibor Gergely exemplify how action drawing tells a story. Pages should be turned slowly, to the end, without reference to the few words. With a second showing of the book and the reading of the words, children will realize how well-chosen words and devices like sound mimicry evoke a dimension of "you are there" experience impossible to pictures alone.

• When using Joan Hanson's *I'm Going to Run Away* and Margaret Wise Brown's *The Runaway Bunny* for contrast, the presenter can make a few quick analyses:
1. Joan Hanson's occasional use of a double-page spread with one picture across two facing pages can be pointed out: "Soon you'll be planning pages like these."
2. Crucial to plot structure is the idea that *every* story "turns around." Both books have an obvious, and similar, pivot in the plot.
3. Looking at both books emphasizes the point that there's no subject under the sun that has not been written; the difference is in how it's done. Capitalize on this observation by guaranteeing that the way each student writes and illustrates a story is going to make it as different as night and day from anyone else's.

All good picture books reinforce these concepts. The nub of truth is understood by all children as they cry or laugh with characters in the story. You know many picture books like these that touch on realities beyond realism. Share them with children before turning them loose to write.

• Here are some books recommended for you to read and use in your classroom:

Booth, David and Kathleen Gould Lundy (2007) *In Graphic Detail: using graphic novels in the classroom.* Rubicon.

Carter, James Bucky (ed.) (2007) *Building Literacy Connections with Graphic Novels.* NCTE.

Cary, Stephen (2004) *Going Graphic.* Heinemann.

Frey, Nancy and Douglas Fisher (2008) *Teaching Visual Literacy.* Corwin.

Green, Judy (1999) *The Ultimate Guide to Classroom Publishing.* Pembroke.

Johnson, Paul (2006) *Get Writing.* Pembroke.

Riddle, Johanna (2009) *Engaging the Eye Generation: visual literacy strategies for the K–5 classroom.* Stenhouse.

Thompson, Terry (2008) *Adventures in Graphics: using comics and graphic novels to teach comprehension, 2–6.* Stenhouse.

Invent Your Plot

Every story takes place somewhere and has a main character with a problem. Your story can take place anywhere you like—underwater, in a haunted house, in outer space, in a backyard—wherever you want. Who or what will your characters be—mermaids, insects, astronauts, aliens, ghosts, a turtle, a chair, a cloud, a stone? Anything, anyone you want.

But be original and invent your own! Don't copy from TV, movies, video games, or other books. Surprise your reader.

Now you need to put those characters in so much difficulty your readers can't imagine how you're going to get them out of it. But you're clever and can make up a neat solution, not always happy, sometimes sad, but something that rings true to readers and makes them say to their friends, "Want to read a good story? Try this one, by (you)."

More on Plot

• Teamwork is frequently part of original writing, especially in media. Two minds listening and making joint judgments enrich the end product. Children benefit from learning cooperation early in a fun activity that springs from the heart.

• Let friends work together, because friends can argue differences of opinion without hurting one another's feelings. A "truer" story is likely to spring from the affection of friends than from two children arbitrarily assigned to work with each other.

• Give the partners ten minutes to sit or walk around the room and talk about who their characters will be, where the action will take place, and what kind of difficulty will arise (no need for resolution yet). No pencil and paper or reference materials yet, just talk and feedback! And no adult interference. It is vital that no one impedes the flow of spontaneous ideas.

• If a team is having serious trouble and not getting anywhere, ask them the basic questions: Who are your main characters? Where does the story take place? What is the problem?

• One in each pair rapidly highlights characters, setting, and difficulty in front of the class, as you jot down the information. The oral reportage is not for your sake. It's to provide an audience for friends whose ingenious ideas are already being reshaped and firmed up in the telling. Hearing others buoys up the less secure students.

• The readings, discussions, and plotting consultations take an hour to 80 minutes.

Character Sketches

Filling out your characters is practice stuff that is fun to do before getting down to the serious business of putting together a whole story.

With pencil on plain paper, draw your characters the way you want them to look: long hair, punk, round head, square body, skinny, plump, tall, short.

Your drawings will not be like a class photograph where everyone looks straight ahead. Of course, we'll want to see your character's face, but draw it from different viewpoints—front, side, back.

Then play around and draw characters in action—bent over, from the back, talking to each other, scolding, mad, laughing. Try giving your new characters different expressions—happy, sad, surprised, angry, frightened, surprised, impatient, sleepy. For tips on how to do this, see the next pages!

Faces

The main parts of the face are the eyes, eyebrows, nose, and mouth.

Use this example to draw the simplest face. Move the dots around. Draw them at the top, at the bottom, at the sides.

These faces say:

Oh!   Hmm!   Hah!   Sniff!   Sob!

Add eyebrows, and now they say:

Oh, no!   No way!   Hello!   Boo Hoo!   Back off!

Expressions and Emotions

Each expression can be taken through the five stages shown here. Try making these expressions in a mirror.

Below are eight different expressions. Those in the first group are the simplest versions. Those in the second group are more complicated because additional lines have been added. Hold up a mirror and use your face to make an expression like each of these.

Experiment with head shapes. They may be ovals, squares, triangles, or pears. Draw some different shapes, adding dots for eyes, etc.

Exaggeration can increase the power of an expression. You can do this by squeezing, stretching, pulling, pushing, lengthening, or shortening a character or object.

Try exaggerating some animal characters or facial expressions—like these!

Character Development

Using stick figures to draw your characters lets you try a variety of poses and actions.

Stick figures are easy to draw and don't take a lot of time, because they have no details.

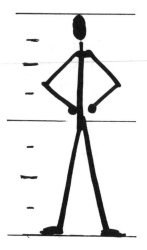   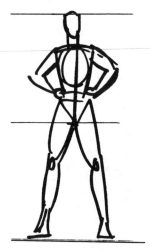

Stick figures can be this simple…

Or have a bit more shape. Torso and limbs are triangular.

Stick figures can even have a skull, ribs, and pelvis.

Once you get the pose, add some form and details. Your character will start to take shape…

A straight up-and-down figures doesn't run as fast as…

… a figure on a diagonal…

… or an even greater diagonal.

I'M PUFFING ALREADY.

LET'S GET MOVING.

This drawing with nine poses was easy to draw and plan using stick figures.

Stick figures aren't just for human characters. Try some animal stick figures.

Let's Get Serious—Research!

When I want to develop a new character for a book or cartoon strip, I do research. Sometimes I look at pictures in magazines and books, and read the articles beside them. I go on the Internet and "Google" a subject.

Sometimes I take my own photographs. These are usually more accurate than someone else's drawings. Or I visit a zoo or pet shop to look at live animals and study how they move, or a museum to see a special display. Then I do many, many, many rough sketches.

Getting information for settings, backgrounds, and props is the same as doing research for a new character. Use photos, magazines, books, scale models, computer images, or actual samples of the things you want to draw. Find out as much as you can.

Practice and patience will help you develop a character that will be your very own. It will be like you—one of a kind!

Here are some suggestions for doing that:

- Move your new character around

- Make it bigger or smaller

- Look at it up close or from far away

- Put it in a particular setting

- Surround it with suitable props

- Try different positions and expressions

Then select your favorite piece for your good sketch.

Plotting the Plot

From our million notes of plots that kids have come up with, here are some that show how far you can let your imagination take you.

Some are exotic:

• on a purple moon, a gigantic sneaker loses its foot

• an alien Santa Claus and a "real" one stage a fight

• Cleopatra, the Sphinx, and a Pyramid have their heads exchanged in a whirlwind

• a baby longs for a house made of apples

• a penguin suffers sunburn on its back

• a frog, a toad, and a dragonfly destroy a city

• three fairies are trapped in a rosebud

• a runaway city drives to New York

• two hungry mice are tossed into space by the moon, when it discovers they think it's made of green cheese

Many are in outer space:

• a child asks his mom if he can go to Mars; she says no; he goes anyway

• robots and boys navigate rival spaceships to Neptune

• three kids, on what's left of Earth, defend it against a robot enemy

• three astronauts save a city in the universe from aliens armed with deadly weapons

• friendly Martians guide lost Earth-children home

Fantasy is popular:

Stories abound of mad scientists, wayward computers, wizards who betray children into hapless crises in complicated time warps. Others, with less sophistication, merrily combine heroic warriors with dinosaurs, and kangaroos with pterodactyls.

Legendary, real, or stuffed animals are all-time favorite heroes:

• Henry Horse wears a dunce cap because his writing is sloppy

• a giraffe is called bad names because of its long neck

• a unicorn and a cat become movie stars

• a rooster talks too much

• a teddy bear is frightened of the dark and something in the closet

• a kangaroo can't hop and a girl helps it learn

• a dolphin and a speckled trout save a fisherman's life

• a mouse doesn't want to go to school

• a lion cub runs away from the circus

Drawing by Drawing

Points of View

How many different ways can you look at an object? Try this: put a soft-drink can, a baseball glove, or a running shoe on the table. Sit on a chair and look at it. Now stand on the chair and look down at it. Try a close look. Then look from across the room. What do you notice close up that you can't see from far away?

Looking from different angles gives you different information about an item. Ask yourself what you want your viewer to see—the overall shape, the lacing on the glove, or maybe just the tear in the leather. Once you decide that, you'll know what angle to choose.

Looking at something from a particular angle is also called choosing a *point of view* or choosing a *focus* for your picture.

A keen observer looks at the world from different angles—from a distance, close up, from overhead or underneath. The point of view influences what a person sees and so it conveys what the author/illustrator is saying to the viewer/reader.

The *size* of a character and *where* you put it on your page help to tell the story. You'll be deciding this when you begin to draw, so examine them carefully now.

Imagine you're a flying camera, moving around a scene to get different points of view.

Look at the pictures in the boxes on pages 22, 24, 25, 27, 28, 33, and 34. A dog, a cat, and a mouse are in each one, but each picture makes you feel differently about them, because of the point of view.

More on Point of View

• Reference to camera angles is an essential preliminary to successful storyboarding. (The main points of view are presented in miniature in the section titled Illustration Ideas, starting on page 83.)

• A display or large posters showing different points of view would be particularly effective at this stage.

• We recommend introducing the *horizontal* point of view first—with characters or objects placed along the "horizon"—and explaining that this is the usual method a child would choose to illustrate an everyday scene. In fact, most children use the horizontal view exclusively.

• We also point out that important figures should be reasonably large and placed in the middle of the scene, not minuscule shapes along the bottom edge of the page or frame.

• Various arrangements of *foreground*, *midground*, and *background* (coming toward the viewer as well as going away) should be illustrated and discussed before any introduction of the dramatic *close-up* or *extreme close-up*, or the more innovative *bird's-eye* and *ant's-eye* viewpoints.

• Each camera angle affects the viewer differently: the coolly horizontal, the angled bird's-eye overview, the ant's-eye underview with its crushing sense of power, or the close-up—most emotional of all.

• Suggest that students watch TV with the sound off. Where is the camera in each shot? Plant the suggestion that students will be varying their own "shots" for the particular effect they want when they plan their illustrations. If you think this is too sophisticated for them, remember that all these children are constantly watching TV, where point of view is choreographed for maximum stimulus. After they have viewed TV for a while with the sound off, their drawings prove how high their visual awareness already is. As young as seven and eight, they are happily varying angles and filling page space with a sense of design.

Horizontal

The most commonly used point of view is the horizontal. A *horizontal* image goes sideways across the page. (A *vertical* image goes up and down.)

Here you see the animals romping along a road. The road is drawn part way up the page. This gives the characters plenty of ground to run across, and they fill the entire space. The road goes *sideways*—along the horizon. That's what "horizontal" means. The horizontal view is used to make a normal, everyday picture, and is calmer than the points of view described next.

Drawing in Layers

Move your characters or objects around using the horizontal view. Bring them forward or move them back. Drawing in layers creates a feeling of distance and space.

Here is an example of how to draw a *layered horizontal* view:

1. Draw a line for the ground. Add two deer near the ground or horizon line.

2. Sketch bushes and trees above the horizon line, so they seem far from the viewer.

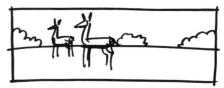

3. Add more hills even higher above the horizon line, or even farther away.

4. Draw a few larger trees and bushes below the horizon line, so they seem close to the viewer.

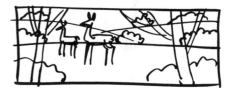

5. Consider sketching a bird or squirrel in these close-up trees.

Notice the different layers in this sailing scene—the dock (or rocks) is shown close to the viewer, the sailboats a little farther away, and the islands farthest away. The actual horizon line is shown—where the water and the sky meet.

The country scene below shows how a horizontal view can have many layers of activity. It can be as simple or as complex as you want it to be.

With a little patience and practice, you will soon be able to give an outdoor scene a feeling of sun, air, and space.

Foreground, Midground, Background

Some points of view are called *foreground* (FG), *midground* (MG), and *background* (BG).

Characters and objects get bigger as they come toward you, and smaller as they go away.

On a page, action usually moves from left to right.

Action Coming Toward You

Here is a simple way of drawing a pathway, a footpath, or a road coming toward you:

1. Inside a frame, draw the horizon as a slightly curving line.

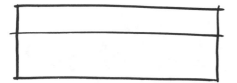

2. On the left side of the horizon line, make a dot.

3. On the bottom line of the frame, slightly inside from each corner, make two dots.

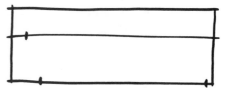

4. Connect these two dots with slightly curving lines, as shown.

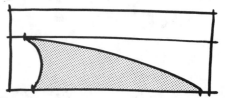

Oh, the poor mouse! The cat and dog are catching up fast! Will it get out of this alive?

To make you feel this anxiety, the illustrator has put the mouse in the *foreground*. It's up close—bigger than the cat and dog.

The road moves at an angle into the distance, with the cat smaller in the *midground* and the dog even smaller in the *background*, both trailing behind the mouse.

Here are some variations:

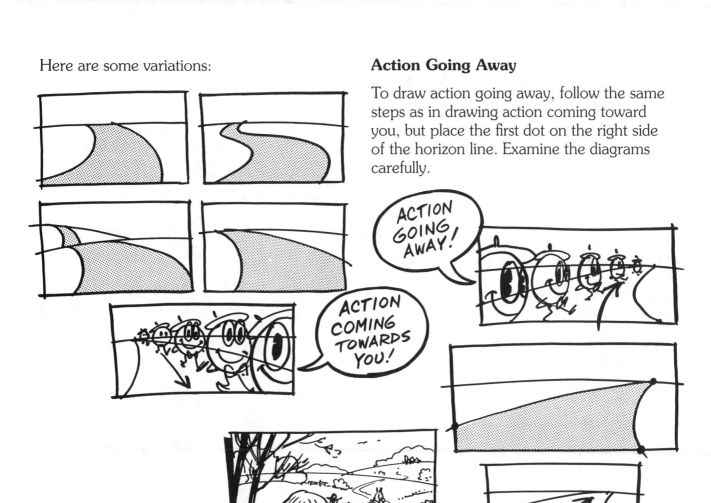

Action Going Away

To draw action going away, follow the same steps as in drawing action coming toward you, but place the first dot on the right side of the horizon line. Examine the diagrams carefully.

Now who is in the foreground? The dog is bigger in this point of view.

Will the dog ever catch up to the others? By drawing the dog up close in the foreground, the illustrator has made you think of it first.

This is what you'll ask yourself before you draw each page in your own book: "Who is the most important in this scene?" Then you'll make that character bigger than the others.

Bird's-Eye View

Imagine you're a bird flying high overhead and looking down at the scene below. What would you see?

Stand up and look down at your feet. Now look at your shoulders. Notice that your shoulders and chest look larger, and your body and legs seem smaller than they really are. Stand on a chair and look down on a friend's head. What do you see? How does this image differ from what you would see when you are standing side by side?

When you draw something from a bird's-eye view, imagine that lines are going down through the subject until they meet at a distant spot. Study the illustration.

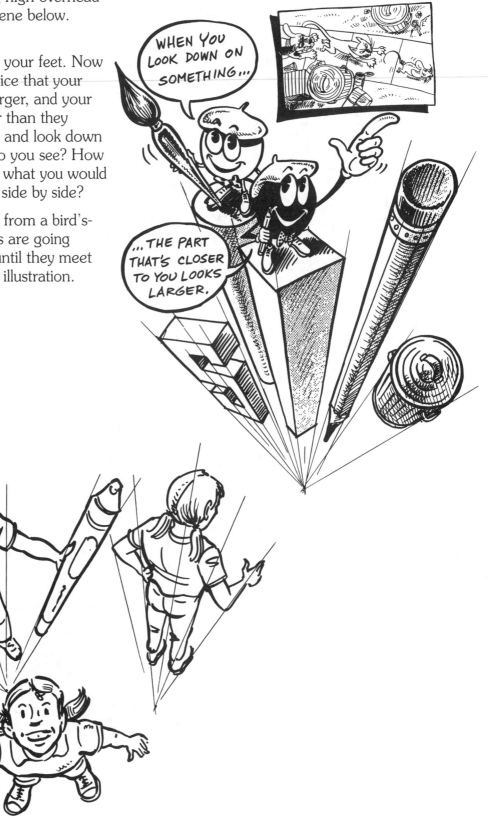

Drawing from a bird's eye view is difficult. Don't get discouraged. You might have to do many rough sketches.

When you start a sketch, draw lightly at first. When you get the main parts "blocked in," darken the outlines.

You're a bird up high looking at the scene below. What a point of view!

Now we know that the dog, the cat, and the mouse are chasing one another on a city street.

When you want to show where the action is taking place and feel that your reader needs an overview, a kind of map of the setting, this is the point of view to use.

Stand on a chair or a table to practice drawing how things look from the top—furniture, your friend's head, a dog's back, or a sleepy cat.

Ant's-Eye View

Imagine you're an ant crawling up your sandy hill. What would you see if you looked up? What would you see if a person walked toward your hill?

Lie down on the floor or under a chair or table. Look up! Interesting, right? A chair looks like a skyscraper. While you are there, ask a friend to stand beside your head. Then look up. An ant's-eye view is dramatic, isn't it?

You're an ant seeing those gigantic feet coming towards you. Are you afraid of that tremendous power? This point of view can be charged with emotion.

Use the ant's-eye view now and again, but not too often, or it will lose its impact.

It's good for variety, especially if you're drawing a sports scene or a long chase, or to show Jack's fear when the beanstalk giant towers over him.

Drawing from the ant's eye view is difficult. Don't be discouraged if your first sketches don't turn out the way you want them to. Patience and practice will help. An ant's-eye view is worth the effort.

Remember, as in the bird's-eye view, draw your lines to meet at a distant point. Study the illustration here.

Drawing Bodies and Heads

Ant's-Eye View

• Draw a cone shape, *point up* (like an ice-cream cone upside down).

• Divide the cone into four equal parts, no need to measure exactly (numbered from bottom to top in the illustration).

• Divide the top quarter in half. This will be the head and shoulder part.

• Have the legs meet at the halfway point.

• Draw the waist in the third quarter.

• Have the feet extend from the bottom line to the top of the first quarter.

Think of the head as an egg shape with the pointed end at the bottom.

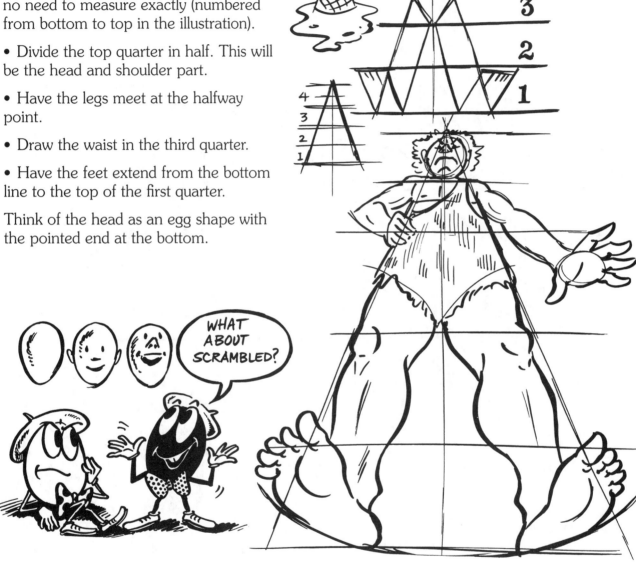

Bird's-Eye View

• Draw a cone, *point down*.

• Divide the cone into four equal parts (numbered from bottom to top in the illustration).

• Divide the second quarter in half. This will be the leg and groin part.

• Have the waist come at the halfway point.

• Draw the head as an oval and have it hang half in and half out of the top quarter.

Special tip for drawing the head:

• Place a mirror below you on a flat surface, such as a table, or stand in front of a wall mirror.

• While looking in the mirror, slowly tilt your head backward.

• Notice how the proportions of your face change until you can see only the underside of your chin, nose, and eyebrows.

• Try the same experiment, tilting your head forward.

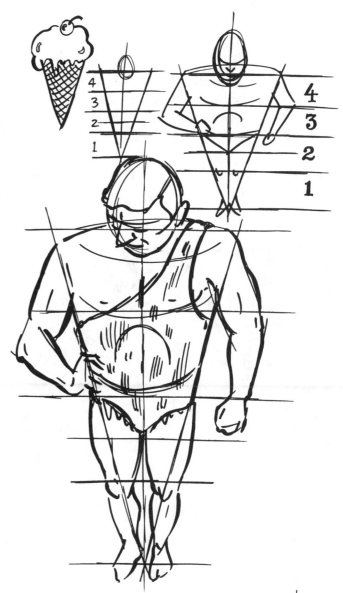

Close-Up

The next pages focus on the close-up view.

The close-up grabs the viewer. Whether on a single frame or page, or as part of a double-page spread, the close-up pulls the viewer into the picture. A face or part of a face in the foreground can't help but get a viewer involved.

Close-ups beg you to ask questions:

• Why are the characters happy? Sad? Worried?

• Where is that horse or car going?

• What's the matter with this baby? Why is it crying so hard?

• Will the poor mouse escape?

Ooooooh!

The close-up is used for your most emotional picture. It interests your reader in only one thing. In this case, it focuses on the mouse. It's worried!

Use the close-up more often than pictures of a character's whole body. It doesn't have to be a face. Maybe it's a hand grabbing a bag, someone's back blocking your view, or a boot kicking a ball to win the match.

Sometimes TV uses the close-up to excite you more than you like, but when you understand how pictures affect the viewer, you may not be too troubled.

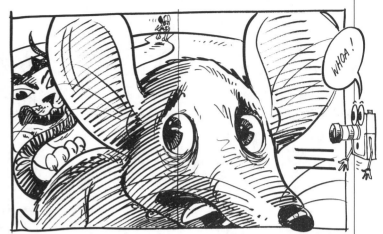

When drawing a close-up, imagine that the character is just entering or leaving the scene. Parts of the body will be *cropped*, or cut off by the border of your frame.

Here are nine small rough sketches showing the same character. Which ones are close-ups?

Extreme Close-Up

Focus very closely on a specific part of an object or character, such as a thumbnail, pupil of an eye, or keyhole, and you have an *extreme close-up.*

What does this extreme close-up of Bad Bart say to you? How does it make you feel?

An extreme close-up demands attention.

An extreme close-up gets you involved. It's in your face! You have to pay attention. An extreme close-up shows only a part of a character. The rest is cropped off the page.

An extreme close-up can be anything:

- a finger pointing in a certain direction
- a hand turning a doorknob
- a raised foot on a sandy beach

This foot shows how it feels to walk along a sandy beach. Notice that the background details contribute to the overall impression.

Remember, an extreme close-up can be almost anything: eyes, a mouth, a foot, a finger, an ear, a key, a pencil, a worm.

Notice that in most of the extreme close-ups on this page a character is involved in the action.

CLICK

A cup and spoon on a table can be an extreme close-up, but…

MAKES ME THIRSTY.

… a hand stirring the spoon makes a more active and interesting close-up.

How about someone drinking from the cup? Now you've got a close-up sequence.

Drawing a Room

A. With two walls and a floor

1. In a rectangle, make a dot in the left half.

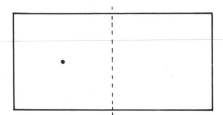

2. Make three dots on the outside borders. With a ruler, draw straight lines to connect these dots.

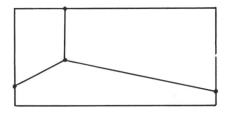

3. Add a door, a rug, and a window.

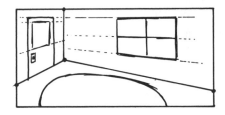

Note: A dotted line or a line drawn very lightly represents an imaginary line.

B. With two walls, a floor, and a ceiling

1. In a rectangle, make two dots in the right half.

2. With a ruler, connect the dots. Then draw lines to the four corners of the rectangle.

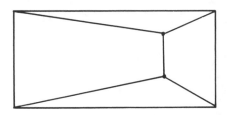

3. Add a door and a window. Angle the top and bottom of both door and window toward the far corner of the room.

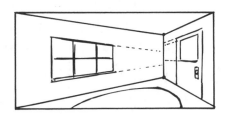

C. With three walls, a floor, and a ceiling

1. In the centre of a rectangle, make a dot.

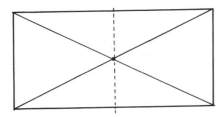

2. Draw a smaller rectangle. With a ruler, draw imaginary lines to connect the dot with the four corners. Then continue the lines outward.

3. Draw the door, window, and furniture with the top and bottom lines going toward the centre dot.

4. Add some characters, painting, lighting fixtures, etc.

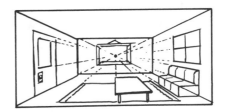

DRAW EVERYTHING LIGHTLY AT FIRST – IN PENCIL.

YOU'LL NEED A RULER FOR THIS WORK.

ARF! ARF! GUESS YOU'RE HUNGRY.

This illustration was made by following Example A. The rug, couch, pillows, curtains, and painting are cutouts from patterned wall paper.

Once you have created a room, you can add objects and characters. Notice that the boy is only partially shown, as if he's walking out of the room. This is an illustration trick! Placing someone or something partially inside the frame creates a feeling that something is happening or is about to happen.

Drawing a House

1. Draw a horizontal line (HL).

2. Draw a square box half above and half below the horizontal line.

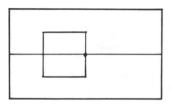

3. At approximately 1-1/2 times the width of the box, make a dot on the righthand side of the line. This is the vanishing point (VP).

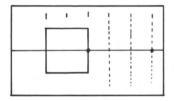

4. Draw lines from the box to the dot.

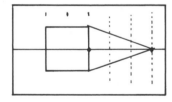

5. Draw the line for the back wall (half the width of the box). Then draw a triangle above the front box.

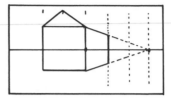

6. Connect the triangle tip to the vanishing point.

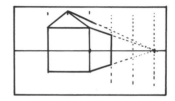

7. Draw the back line of the roof. This should be at the same angle as the front of the roof.

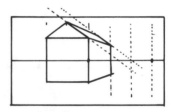

8. Add the finishing touches—trees, sidewalk, etc.

FOR THIS WORK YOU'LL NEED A RULER. REMEMBER TO DRAW LIGHTLY.

Drawing in perspective is difficult. Copy these samples and keep practicing.

What makes this illustration effective?

Dark objects placed in the foreground! The tree, fence, and man are simple shapes cut out of dark paper and glued on top of the background drawing. The background drawing was done with different kinds of lines and shading. The children and the horse were cut out of paper.

This illustration was done in layers. An easy way to work!

The Rough Sketch

To save time, do a quick sketch before you start an illustration. This will help you think through what you want in your picture. If you don't like your first sketch, do another. Fill a page with quick sketches until you are happy with the results. Remember, a rough sketch is supposed to be *rough*. It should be done quickly and have no detail, because it is not meant to be your good copy.

Here is how to do a rough sketch of an elephant:

• First, study the animal (pictures or real life) carefully. Look at its basic shapes and angles. Where do you see circles, ovals, triangles, squares, or rectangles?

• Draw these shapes quickly. Keep your outline simple. You can add detail later.

Do as many rough sketches as possible on one piece of paper. This will help you see all the various shapes, angles, and positions at the same time.

Then select your best or favorite work for your good sketch. This is still a quick, rough drawing, but it captures the idea or subject accurately.

Whether you use a sketchbook or single sheets of paper, you need some system of storing your sketches. A filing folder would do for the single sheets.

Thinking in Thumbnails

You started with rough sketches, filling the page with your drawings. Now you need to concentrate on small, quick drawings with no detail. These are called *thumbnail sketches*. Thinking in thumbnails means thinking small!

Drawing small has many advantages over drawing full-size:

• It takes less time.

• It saves paper and space.

• It allows the artist to plan the drawing quickly.

• It makes changes and redrawing easy.

• It prevents the artist from adding unnecessary detail because there is less room.

This last point is important. People who like to draw just itch to add detail. Of course this is good, but not at the planning stage. The problem is that, once you've done a detailed drawing, you get attached to it. You don't want to change anything, even though you know it needs improving.

Before drawing a thumbnail sketch, ask yourself these questions:

• What is the most important thing to focus on? The characters? The setting? Both? An object? The action? Remember, you haven't much room.

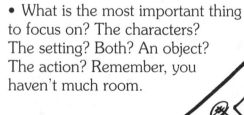

For a Comic

You can plan your page layout with thumbnail sketches.

44

- Which character is the most important?

- What part of the setting is the most important?

- What is going on? What are the characters doing?

First draw a small rectangle and do your sketch inside. If you need more space, no problem, draw outside the border. Then draw a new border.

A border, or frame, helps to isolate the action.

Characters and objects exist outside the border.

You can move a border in (zoom in) to get more drama and to eliminate unwanted background.

Storyboarding

By now you should have hundreds of sketches of your characters, settings, backgrounds, and props. Are you ready to use them in a story?

Why use a storyboard?

• A storyboard allows you to plan a thumbnail (see page 44), rough copy (see page 42) version of your complete story from front to back cover.

• With stick figures or circle characters, as I have used in this book, it's easy to draw.

• It can be done quickly and shared with others.

Perhaps you know the ending you want for your story, but haven't quite figured out how to begin. So draw the ending first. The beginning is often the hardest part, so fill in the middle next and do the beginning last. This method can help prevent a long-winded introduction and get your reader to the exciting part quickly.

A storyboard has pages side by side, as in the pages of a book: 4/5, 6/7, 8/9, etc. These pages face each other and are called a *double-page spread*.

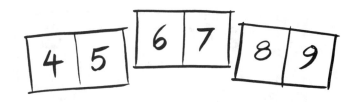

REMEMBER, THIS IS ROUGH COPY DRAWING.

An illustration can…

• stretch across a double-page spread

• go across a page and a bit

• be a single-page illustration with the other side used for words

• be a small *spot* illustration (a square, rectangle, or circle) with words on the same page

Do not write the words of your story at this stage. Instead, draw short lines to show where the words will go later. Sound effects, however, can be included. *Boom!*

Three easy steps:

• Plan your story. Think about how you want it to begin and end. What will be the high point of interest?

• Sketch the complete storyboard quickly with stick figures or circle characters and no detail.

• Draw short horizontal lines to indicate where words will go later.

Materials You'll Need

• Storyboards on white paper. See pages 87–91.

• Pencils

• Erasers

• Paper

DON'T STOP THE VISUAL FLOW.

From Thumbnails...

Let's develop some thumbnail sketches for the story Little Red Riding Hood. As we do so, we'll include what we have learned about points of view (pages 20–37).

First, ask some questions:

• How does the story start?

• What is the most exciting or interesting part?

• What are the different settings?

• What character or scene will I sketch? Red Riding Hood? Grandma? The Wolf? The forest?

Sometimes an image just pops into your head. That's a good place to start. Draw it. Do a few thumbnail sketches.

Remember, composition includes all the parts of your illustration (characters, setting, point of view, type) and how they fit together.

Play with the composition! Move things around. Bring them forward; move them back; move them up or down.

Here are some possibilities for using your knowledge of points of view:

• Red Riding Hood skipping through the woods to Grandma's house (close-up).

• skipping (horizontal)

• skipping toward the forest (bird's-eye view)

• the Wolf hiding behind a tree (foreground)

• the Wolf jumping out of the bed to grab Red Riding Hood (foreground)

• the Wolf—"Grandma, what big teeth you have!" (close-up, even extreme close-up of the unbrushed teeth)

Remember, you are a flying movie camera with a zoom lens. Move in. Pull back. Change angles and shapes until the characters look right.

... To Storyboard

A variety of thumbnail sketches allow you to explore different ideas and point of view for any moment in your story. These sketches show Red Riding Hood skipping along happily. Which one do you choose to start the story? You might even choose two to really set the tone on pages 4/5 and 6/7: a distant short to start, and then a semi-closeup view.

Storyboarding a Graphic Novel or Comic

Graphic novels and comics often use more images to tell a story than a picture book does. A single moment or action in a comic might be shown from many viewpoints; in a picture book, you would choose just one view.

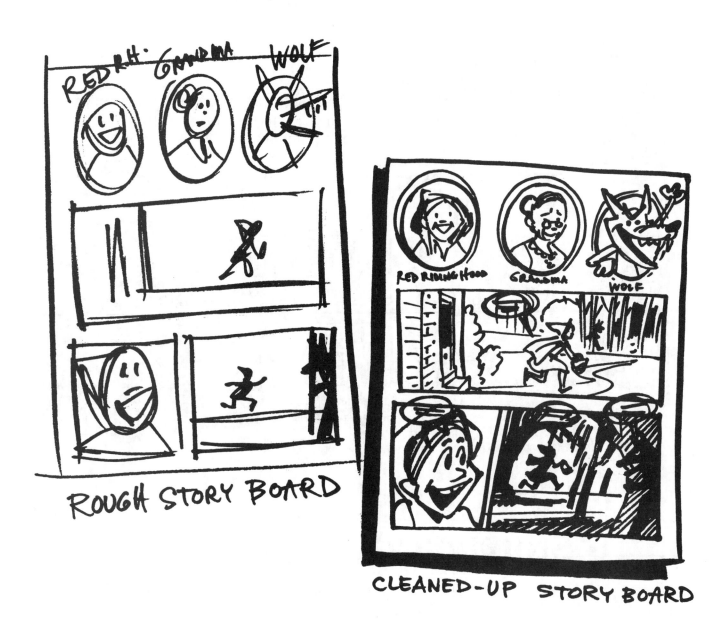

ROUGH STORY BOARD

CLEANED-UP STORY BOARD

More on Storyboarding

The storyboard, which you can copy from the one provided on page 88, is a grid of 28 squares or frames, the first representing the front cover of a book, the last, the back cover. Intervening frames are paired for double-page spreads, with a wide black line between each pair, signifying the all-important page turn. The frames numbered #4 to #24 are the actual frames in which students draw their story. The rest, as shown, will be endpapers, copyright and dedication page, and title page.

• Mention the suspense of a page turn. This is particularly apparent in a pattern book where the answer to a repeated question isn't given until the page is turned and a hundred possibilities for it have already been prompted.

• We suggest students put a small X on frames #12/#13 to indicate their story needs to be at its most difficult here (or somewhere in this line of frames). The worst has happened. How will the characters survive or solve their problems?

• They can begin drawing story action in frames #4 and #5, or start at the dilemma point and go through to the end before tackling the opening. Some catch on readily to this upheaval of usual progression, some are alarmed, but all are made aware, simply by its mention, that openings must not be labored.

• Offer little guidance, if any, during the initial storyboarding. You'll help with the editing when the storyboard is finished.

• Don't draw on children's work unless you ask and they say it's okay. Otherwise, demonstrate on a separate piece of paper or on a blank storyboard.

• Don't tamper with their story ideas, unless you sense total confusion or lazy-brain. The adult role is to preserve the originality of thought by helping children express it to maximum effect.

• To avert the disappointment of a lost story, we recommend at this stage the photocopying of a master set of the completed storyboards.

Using a Storyboard

Now it's time for action! It's time to draw our plot on a storyboard, but you're not going to write your story until *after* you've drawn it.

By the time you've pencilled pictures quickly on the storyboard and, later, done your book mock-up, you'll have so much feeling for your characters that the words you'll choose then will make your book come alive for your reader.

With a pencil, swiftly draw the action of your characters as circle or stick figures, beginning in frames #4 and #5 and ending with frame #24, the end of your story. Frames #1 to #3 will be used later for special information.

You could even begin drawing where your characters are in their worst trouble, probably by frames #12 and #13. Finish from there to frame #24 and then go back to #4 and fill in the beginning. This keeps you from telling us more than we need to know about your characters early in the story.

This is storyboarding your plot, not beautiful art, so without adding details of hair and clothes and background, you'll easily finish storyboarding in an hour or less.

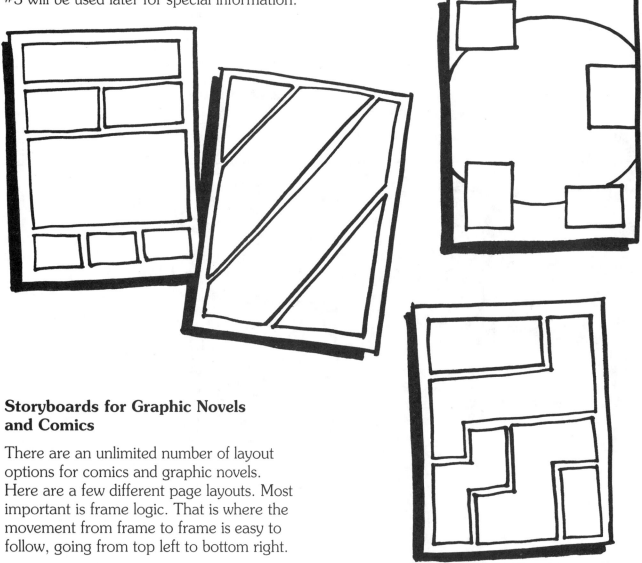

Storyboards for Graphic Novels and Comics

There are an unlimited number of layout options for comics and graphic novels. Here are a few different page layouts. Most important is frame logic. That is where the movement from frame to frame is easy to follow, going from top left to bottom right.

Hints for Storyboarding

• It's action you're drawing, not talking heads. Make bodies show what's happening by the way you make them move and relate to each other

• Use a *variety of views*—bird's-eye, ant's-eye, and lots of big close-ups. (These points of view are explained in Stage 3.)

• Decide where you want an illustration and where the words will go.

• Because it gives more power to spread a drawing over facing pages, you might sometimes want to use the *double-page spread*.

• Think about the suspense of a *page turn*.

• It's your characters that people will care about, so make them large. Don't draw teensy figures along the bottom of the frame. Put them higher up and fill the space!

• Most importantly, jump into your story feet first. Your reader doesn't want to hear about the alarm clock going off, admirable teeth brushing, or saying goodbye to Mom. Capture interest by providing trouble and complications as soon as possible.

• And, of course (does it need to be said?), *no words* go on the storyboard, just lines to indicate where they will go later.

| Done?
Put it away.
That's enough
for a busy day. |

Editing Your Storyboard

Now that you've been away from your storyboard for a while, look at it as if someone else had done it. You'll see places where you can change, or edit, your story to make it clear. These changes will be easy to do because you used a pencil for your first work.

Book Mock-Up

The book mock-up is a page-by-page rough copy of your book based on your storyboard. It has pages the same proportion as those in the full-color book you will do later. The characters are still circle or stick figures—with no detail. Words are not used, although lines may be drawn to indicate where they will go later. Major shapes and important objects are outlined.

Take seven sheets of paper 21.5 cm x 35.5 cm (8.5" x 14"). Then fold them in half and put them inside each other, as shown in the diagram.

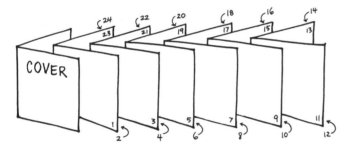

The folded outer sheet is the cover, front and back. The six folded inner sheets are the pages. Number these 1 to 24, as shown in the diagram. Pages 12/13 would be the centrefold. It's important that you number pages in the correct sequence

Don't fasten them, because after you have numbered them, you can take them apart to draw on.

WHAT AN EXCITING DOUBLE-PAGE SPREAD.

You'll use a pencil for drawing your book mock-up, as you did for your storyboard, because this also is fast-pencil work, or quick work, that you might want to change later.

As a guide, prop up the revised storyboard and your pages of rough sketches.

Begin to draw on pages 4 and 5 of the book mock-up to match the pictures on frames #4 and #5 of your storyboard. Or you can start around pages 12 and 13, in the middle of the book. Block in major shapes and important objects—ground, trees, buildings, flowers—as well as your characters. Continue from here to page 24, and then go back and fill in the opening pages. Pages 1 to 3 will be used later for special things like title, dedication, and publishing information.

Remember to transfer a double-page spread on your storyboard to two pages in the book mock-up. If you don't do this, the pages that follow will not be in the carefully planned order of your storyboard.

You are still doing only outlines of the sketches you designed earlier. Don't do details. Save these for the final book you'll soon be coloring. Also, don't do covers yet and don't add any words.

Books and comics come in a variety of sizes and shapes. Will your book be vertical, horizontal, or square? It's up to you. The paper most readily available is 8.5" x 11" (21.5 cm x 28 cm) or 8.5" x 14" (21.5 cm x 35.5 cm). This paper is folded in half, and the top portion can be cut off to give the correct shape.

Materials You'll Need

For a 24-page book (plus covers, endpapers, publisher's information page, and title page).

• Seven sheets of newsprint or bond paper; 21.5 cm x 35.5 cm (8.5" x 14")

• Pencils

• Erasers

• Rulers

More on the Book Mock-Up

• An edited storyboard catapults author/illustrators into a rough copy, called the mock-up. It is the same format that the finished book will be. In this case, seven pieces of paper, folded, become a 24-page book (plus covers, endpapers, publisher's information page, and title page).

• This is fast-pencil work, loose and rapid, without words, images filling the space, adapting the pictures on storyboard frames to full book pages. The emphasis is on design, seeing the unity of a double-page spread or, if there are single-page drawings, keeping an eye on how they balance the work on the facing page.

• Discourage time-consuming detail. Only major shapes and important objects are outlined. Just like the storyboard, the book mock-up will be edited later.

• Editing the book mock-up is conducted in the same way as editing the storyboard, in private sessions. Since the storyline was firmly established when the storyboard was edited, the book mock-up deals with visual placement.

Design a Visual Surprise

Every page of a picture book should be a visual surprise! Will it be a close-up of a face, or a super close-up of only one eye? A distant view? An ant's-eye or bird's-eye view? A detailed landscape or cityscape, showing all the color and texture of the countryside or city?

Remember to leave enough space for the words of your story. Where the type, or text, is placed is important to the overall flow of the book.

Facing pages are seen together by the reader. If one illustration goes across both pages, it is drawn as a double-page spread. But when each page has a separate image, its design must still be planned in relation to the page it faces. This makes for smooth continuity in viewing as well as reading.

Editing Your Book Mock-Up

• Do the drawings fill up the space?

• Do important characters need to be made bigger than others?

• Are the characters well up from the bottom of the page?

• Do the bodies show action and relate to each other?

• Are double-page spreads exciting?

• Do single-page designs balance the drawings and word spaces on the facing page?

• Ask a friend to tell you the story based on your illustrations. This kind of buddy editing will alert you to possible problems in your storyline.

Illustration Styles

• Various uses of foreground, midground, and background.

• Different ways of viewing three objects—person, tree, house.

• Whatever is in the foreground influences the drama of the page.

• Where text is placed affects the overall flow of your book.

Planning the Design and Type

Now is the time to start thinking about the text or type to be included with your illustrations—the captions for your pictures.

Where to Put the Type

Where the type is placed depends on

- how much there is

- how large or elaborate it is

- whether it is for a picture book, a graphic novel, or a comic strip

Type usually goes at the top of the page, but it can go anywhere you wish—as long as you have left space for it. One place it should *not* go is across the *gutter* from a lefthand page to the righthand page across from it. The reason for this is that, when a book is bound, letters in the gutter can get lost, or not line up. The same goes for small details in drawings.

> THE GUTTER IS THE DIVISION BETWEEN TWO PAGES.

> I ONCE KNEW A WORD THAT GOT LOST IN THE GUTTER AND WAS NEVER SEEN AGAIN.

Word Balloons

Word balloon logic is about where you place word balloons. It's most important to keep in mind that we read from left to right, and from top to bottom. Sequential dialogue has to follow this order. To make it easier to read, lettering in word balloons is almost always in capital letters.

A LOGICAL SEQUENCE

CONFUSING - NOT CERTAIN WHAT TO READ

A LOGICAL SEQUENCE

A Full-Color Book

This is it! Now that you've done the fast planning with your storyboard and book mock-up, you can take all the time you want putting in the details in your full-color book.

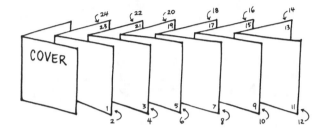

Fold seven sheets of heavy paper the same size as you used for the book mock-up. Put them inside each other and number the pages made up of the six inside sheets 1 to 24, as shown. The seventh sheet on the outside makes the book covers.

Begin coloring on pages 4 and 5, and follow the plan of your book mock-up. Check your page sequence as you go—you don't want your final book to get mixed up. Remember that pages 1 to 3 will be used later for special information.

Materials You'll Need

• Seven sheets of colored manila or plain cartridge paper, same size as book mock-up

• Colored markers: find markers that don't bleed through the page

• Pencil crayons: for fine detail

• Paint and brushes: let paint dry before continuing

• Big and little cans of water

• Lots of newspapers to protect surfaces and floors

• Crayons or oil pastels: colors will melt if pages are laminated

More on the Full-Color Book

Storyboarding is for all children, whatever their artistic or writing skills. Its aim is expression, not achievement compared to someone else's. Expect a mess, but watch the enthusiasm, concentration, and sheer pleasure children experience as they set to their tasks with meticulous vigor. When the ban on detail is lifted, self-directed perfectionism takes over.

• Have on hand an abundant supply of coloring and collage materials, the greater variety the better.

• Supply each child with a book of good quality manila or cartridge paper, the same size and with the same number of pages as the book mock-up, plus covers.

• To avoid later mix-ups, have students number the pages immediately, matching the numbers exactly with those in the book mock-up.

• The medium is indeed the message. What we are trying to avoid is handing students the familiar piece of lined paper and saying, "Now go to it!" Lined paper tends to make them revert to "once upon a time … and then … and then." But if they start with a storyboard, and then take more lined paper, on their own they put down the page numbers to match the storyboard. Now they're keeping a focus, reflected in acute language.

• We live in a community where children of many cultural backgrounds arrive constantly. Few can speak English. All can draw. They are encouraged to write the drawn story in their own language, if they wish.

Shading for Reality

"How does an artist make things look real?"

To make an object or character look real, an artist shades with tone—from light to dark.

Shading is done with lines, dots, and dashes.

Lines can…

• wiggle, wave, jump, twist turn

• be long or short, thick or thin

• be horizontal, vertical, or diagonal

• be close together or far apart

Dots and dashes can…

• be small or large

• have bumps or hooks

• be close together or far apart

The last item in each list is the key. The magic of shading comes from drawing lines, dots, or dashes close together or far apart. That's it!

Try shading. Draw some short horizontal lines. Put some close together, others far apart. See the difference?

Draw freehand. You'll get good at it in no time.

Cross-hatching is another way to create tones or shades. These are lines that cross over each other at different angles— horizontal, vertical, diagonal. When the lines are far apart, they create a light tone. When they are close together, they create a dark tone.

Practice cross-hatching. Begin with horizontal lines; then draw diagonal lines. Draw the diagonal lines, as shown, at a 45° angle to the horizontal lines. Draw the vertical lines last.

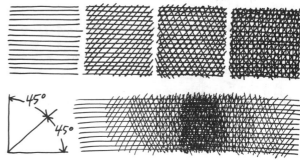

Light and Shadow

Have you ever stood in front of a mirror with a flashlight under your chin? I used to do that when I was ten years old. The light would catch the bottom of my chin, cheeks, nose, and eyebrows. I would practice making spooky faces. Even today, when I need to draw an unusual or different expression, I sometimes pull out a flashlight.

WHEW! I NEED SOME SHADE.

Shadows help to make objects or characters look solid. They show when something is still or moving, sitting or floating, close by or far away. They also tell you the time of day.

The best way to learn how to draw shadows is to observe shadows and draw what you see.

On a sunny day, go for a walk with a friend and concentrate only on shadows—your own shadow or that of your friend, a cat, a dog, a building, a tree, or a bouncing ball. The last item might be the most surprising of all. What do you see?

The direction of light affects the length of the shadow. Morning, afternoon, and evening light are different. How does a noonday shadow differ from a late-afternoon shadow?

Another good way to learn about light and shadow is to create a *still life* scene. Arrange some books, fruit, jars, containers, boxes, or pots on a flat surface. Observe the shadows. Then draw the still life, including the shadows, of course.

Knowing where and how to use shadows will help you create a sense of drama in your illustrations. Shadows add mood, suspense, mystery, danger, and a feeling of weight.

Using Collage Illustration for a Picture Book

Cut-and-Paste Collage

Are you one of those people who always says, "No way! I can't draw!"? Well, don't be discouraged. Brushes and paint, pencils and paper aren't the only way to make pictures. Try scissors, glue, and a pile of old magazines. This stage explores ideas for cutting and arranging colored paper and magazine pictures to create dynamic illustrations for your picture book. Anyone can do that!

A good way to use color is with cut-and paste designs. You can cut shapes from paper to represent your characters instead of drawing them. Use wallpaper samples, construction paper, or illustrations or photographs. Then past them onto colored cut-out backgrounds.

You can also do collage with cloth or curly wool or buttons or spaghetti or toothpicks… Paste them on for hair or fur or clothing or machines…

Experiment with pop-ups, see-through pages, hinged windows and doors, or accordion folds. And mix and match any of these. It's your own inventive, original book.

It's important to remember that all the things that have come before on character and plot development, point of view and composition, all apply equally to this illustration form. Collage allows for objects, shapes, patterns, and characters—many things your have drawn—to be cut out of paper. All those things still should be there, but collage just gets rid of the need for everything to be drawn.

Materials You'll Need

- Scissors
- Glue, glue stick, paste, sticky tape
- Colored construction paper
- Wallpaper samples, gift wrap
- Pictures from magazines or the Internet
- Cotton balls, cloth scraps
- Egg cartons
- Pasta shapes
- Wool, embroidery cotton, string, cord
- Pencils—regular and colored
- Colored markers
- Oil pastels

More on Collage

For many children, collage provides a rich outlet for artistic expression.

- Remember that the mock-up they follow has already been edited for balanced design.

- Whole shapes cut from paper now represent characters; exotic backgrounds are derived from fancy papers or photos; even pop-ups, see-throughs, pull-downs, or foldouts may be added.

- The tactile manipulation of cotton, artificial fur, wools, etc. for small detail continues to deepen the attachment to "my book."

Fun-Tastic Collages

Try different styles and materials. Experiment! Explore! Change!

For example, unusual illustrations and lettering can be created by tearing paper. This produces a ragged, fuzzy, uneven quality. Try doing an illustration using torn paper in layers.

Here is an example of experimentation. The original sun was drawn with black marker on orange paper. Some people liked it, but I thought it needed movement and vitality. So I cut the image into horizontal strips, separated them slightly, and moved the pieces to the left and right. Then I glued them onto a lighter or contrasting background.

Here is a variety of suns. Try this approach with sketches of dogs, cats, tress, cloud, chairs—anything you wish.

Cutouts for Starters

"I can't draw cars, or buildings, or ships, or even trees! I can't draw anything!" Sound familiar? If you can't draw, don't let that stop you from doing fun-tastic illustrations. Get a good pair of scissors, a pile of old magazines, and cut out your illustrations.

Of course, you don't just cut out anything. You will need to browse through many magazines to find the exact images you want. And don't forget words and lettering—these will come in handy.

Combine your images with drawings, words, and other cutout paper shapes.

Cut and Paste with Patterned Paper

Patterned paper (wallpaper, gift wrap, even patterned cloth) looks fantastic when cut out and used in a design.

Careful planning will help you achieve a colorful and dramatic collage illustration. Remember to follow your rough sketches and storyboard.

• With lines, striped, or dotted patterns, arrange the angles so there is a variety of horizontal, vertical, and diagonal directions.

• Don't glue down any of your illustration until all the pieces are cut out and assembled. When you are satisfied with the arrangement, you can glue them down.

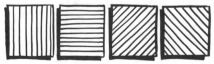

Simple Cutout Shapes

Simple shapes can be cut out of colored or patterned paper.

- If you don't like your first attempt, do it again.

- Use colored or patterned paper.

- Draw detail on the cutout shapes.

- Try some of these: frog, rabbit, cat, dog, tree, shoe, gingerbread person, hand, foot.

- Keep the shapes simple and bold so they will stand out.

For this jungle scene, the monkey's tail and lion's head were cut out once but used twice. Can you find them both?

For underwater scenes, try to convey the movement of water by cutting paper into wavy strips and separating them slightly.

Faces with Cutouts and Markers

To construct the simplest face, like MR. BRISTLE, follow these steps:

1. Cut out eyes, eyebrows, and a moustache from colored construction paper. Make them wild!

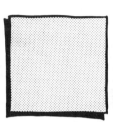  

2. Place them on a background. Don't glue them down yet!

3. Draw the outline of a head. Don't forget the ears. Leave space for a neck and part of a body.

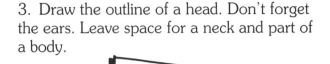

4. Add glasses, a hat, a tie, and whatever else you want. Cut these out of different colors or paper. Add them to the outlined head and glue everything down.

To create a character like MS. FRIZZ, draw a face outline on your background. Use wool for her hair and a paper doily for a collar.

Special Effects with Cutouts

Create water or underwater scenes by pasting plain cutout shapes of fish, sailboats, motorboats, canoes, ships, or swimmers. Then draw details. Try airplanes, rockets, or spaceships; cars, trucks, motorcycles; daffodils and tulips.

Use layers for special effects:

• Shade and create texture on background paper.

• Lay cutouts on top of paper.

• Draw on top of cutouts.

• Paint on top of background paper.

• Glue or tape leaves, buttons, cotton, macaroni, etc. to background paper.

Cutout Letters and Numbers

Use cutout letters for titles on book covers and for special effects (sounds, for example).

Follow these steps:

1. Choose a color that suits your illustration or story.

2. Cut strips of paper high enough for the letters needed. A little extra length allows for mistakes or miscalculations. The strip keeps all the letters the same height.

3. Cut the strips into blocks for letters of different widths. Remember that an M is wider than an O, and that an I is thinner than an F.

4. Note the different ways of cutting the letter A, depending on whether a block or a triangular shape is desired.

5. Cut "closed-in" letters (A, B, D, O, P, Q, and R) without folding the paper. The outline letters below show where the scissors have overcut their mark. This is good because it ensures that the inside or enclosed pieces will fall out easily.

The overcuts, by the way, will not show up when the letter parts are pressed together and glued down, as seen below.

ABDOPQR

Block Lettering

1. Block lettering is the easiest shape to cut out with scissors.

ABCDEF
GHIJKLM
NOPQRS
TUVWXYZ
& ?!.,
12345
67890

2. Here are some different ways to cut the letter S. (These cutting techniques apply to all letters.)

3. Remember to vary the size and to use lowercase (small) letters for contrast.

AND and

and

Hand-Made Patterned Papers

Create your own patterned papers. The following suggestions work best if you use water-based paints on shiny or glossy paper.

• *Splatter* paint using an old toothbrush or stiff-bristled paint brush.

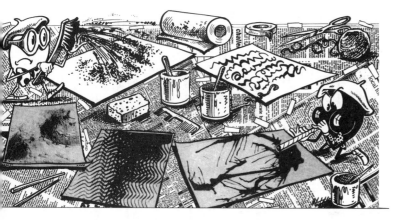

• *Blow* paint with a drinking straw. (Don't inhale!)

• *Print* patterns with cutout styrofoam shapes, a carved potato, or a piece of string.

• *Smear* paint with a rag or sponge.

• *Scribe* lines and patterns into wet paint with a chopstick, fork, or old comb.

• *Squish* paint between two pieces of paper.

• *Cut out* stencils, especially if you want to repeat an image.

Before you start, cover the work area with lots of newspaper. Tape the newspaper down so it doesn't move around. Have a supply of paper towels or rags ready in case of spills.

Making Squish-and-Print Patterned Paper

1. Pour two or three colors of paint in the middle of a piece of glossy paper.

2. Place another piece of glossy paper on top. Squish the paint around. It's all right if some paint oozes out the sides.

3. Hold the two sheets firmly by one end. Pull back the top sheet slowly in sections, bit by bit. This will pull the paint into a pattern.

4. Separate the two sheets and let them dry.

TRY THE OTHER FUN-TASTIC TECHNIQUES!

To use your paper for cutouts: with a pencil, lightly draw an outline (frog, cat, dog, house, etc.) and cut it out. On the cutout, draw details with a pencil, marker, crayon, etc.

It's a Book!

Writing Your Story

At last—words!

You can write a first draft of your story before or after finishing the full-color book, as you wish.

You can use a blank storyboard or plain paper, but either way, remember to match up your words with the number of the page on which they will appear.

Using a storyboard keeps you from saying too much. It forces your mind to choose what matters most. If you are writing a graphic novel or comic strip, you will have to decide what goes in the speech balloons, and what goes in the captions. If you are writing a picture book, you will be writing full sentences, not just a few words in balloons.

You have drawn your book to show the action so your words don't need to say "and then… and then." What they need to say is how your characters feel as the plot evolves—what they smell, what they hear; how foods taste; how scared, mixed-up, happy, angry, or sad they are.

Words should make your readers feel that they're actually living inside your story.

Editing Your Story

• Read your story out loud and change words as you hear their rhythm and sound.

• Show your story to someone who can help you with spelling and punctuation.

When it's finally the way you want it, you can hand print it neatly on the pages of your full-color book, or you can type it on a computer and paste cut-out sections of the print-out on the correct pages.

Lettering Styles

Each style of lettering, or typeface, has its own personality. Letters can be plain, decorative, sharp, squat, thick, thin, sad, happy.

A particular word can make you think of it in a certain way—like the words shown here. Create a typeface to suit the words on your book cover.

Your Book Title and Cover

Your title makes people want to open your book. It should tease them to look inside.

On this page is a list of terrific titles other kids have made up. Some are questions. They don't give away the plot. They don't use characters' names or the overworked "Mystery of…" or "Trouble with…" They're all more original than that. And so will yours be when you take time to think seriously about its importance.

BOOGIE UNDER THE BED

THE GREAT HONEY SEARCH

GREEN SANTA CLAUS

WHAT HAPPENED TO MY TAIL?

THE HOUSE THAT SCARES PEOPLE

WHAT? WHAT? DINOSAURS! DINOSAURS!

THE COMPACT GENIE

DIVE IN THE SEA

WAS THAT A UFO?

DARK CASTLE

THE NEW FRIENDSHIP

NIGHT JUGGLER

Designing a Cover

Now that you have dreamed up a super title, you can design your cover. As with posters, there are two things to keep in mind about book covers:

• The main words should be large and easy to read.

• The illustration, if there is one, should be bold, bright, dramatic, and to the point.

A cover usually has the following:

• the title

• the names of the author and illustrator

• an illustration (sometimes the main character or a scene from the story)

A cover can give a hint of what the book is about. It can tease the reader, but should not give away the plot or storyline.

Both the cover design and illustration, if there is one, should suit the book. Is the book exciting, strange, quiet, serious, or mysterious? Is it a picture book or a graphic novel/comic book?

Remember to try different points of view—horizontal, close-up, ant's-eye, bird's-eye. Move objects and characters around. Bring them forward; move them back.

Each of these six examples gives a different feeling of what's going on:

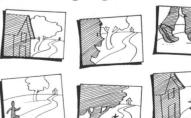

Materials You'll Need

- Cardboard, bristol board, heavy construction paper, vinyl wallpaper, thin plywood, or wallboard

- Stapler with a long handle

- Glue or glue sticks

- Tape (preferably book-binding) in different colors

- Wool, string, cord, or even dental floss

A binder and laminating machine would be useful, but are not really necessary.

More on the Finished Book

- All children have had a title in their minds, even before they knew how their story would end, but we have discouraged them from putting it on the book mock-up or final cover. Until now. Because with the book inside, they can conjure up a better one. Ask them to scan library shelves and note which titles make them want to look inside the book. Whatever the content, the title has done its job—teased them in.

- Suggest that the cover design be planned as a *grand finale* to sum up the whole story.

- The inside of the front cover and its facing page, as well as the inside of the back cover, are reserved as endpapers for those who still want to adorn their books. This is definitely optional. These can be abstract or geometric patterns, drawn or done in collage. They might incorporate an image symbolizing the theme or setting of the story; for example, sailboats in a seagoing tale, weird aliens in a space story.

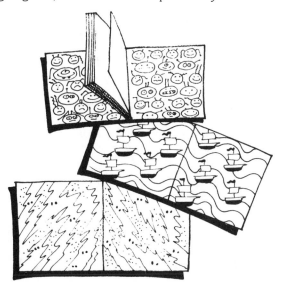

- To make a protective outside cover, these are the steps:

1. Cut an endpaper sheet the same height as the content pages but slightly wider.

2. With string, dental floss, or wool, sew the content pages to the endpaper sheet, as shown.

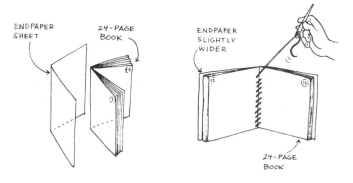

3. Cut a cover sheet the same height as the endpaper sheet but slightly wider, and fold it in half.

4. Glue the outside of the endpaper sheet (with content pages attached) to the inside of the cover.

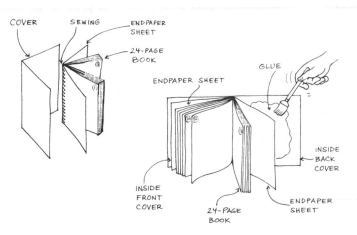

- Plan a gala publishing party at which the author/illustrators can show and read their books to parents, friends, classmates, and children from other classes.

Finishing Touches

About the Author/Illustrator: Everyone wants to know about the author and illustrator of a picture book, graphic novel, or comic strip. You are now an author and an illustrator with your photograph on page 1 or the back cover (inside or outside). That will please your reading public.

Copyright Page: Publisher's information and dedication go on page 2. A small c in a circle, followed by your name and the date—© The Author, Year—establishes your copyright. This custom tells your reader that you own the story and/or the illustrations.

In large letters, print *Dedicated to*, or *I dedicate this book to*, or simply *Dedication:*, followed by the name of someone you care for.

Title Page: The title will go on page 3, which had to stay blank until your title was chosen. Now you print your title on it in the same lettering style as on the cover. Or just print it in large, clear letters, along with your name as author and illustrator. You don't need a picture here.

Endpapers: You can put a repeated design related to the theme of your story on the inside of the front cover or back cover, or both.

Cover: If you have access to a laminating machine, that would be ideal for protecting your book. But if you haven't, you can make a sturdy outside cover of cardboard or bristol board, heavy construction paper, vinyl wallpaper, or even very thin plywood. Cover it with cloth, felt, burlap, gift wrap, mesh from bags used for fruit or vegetables, nylon from stockings, road maps, or newspapers. The choice is yours.

Binding: You have all these fantastic pages of pictures and story, and you have a protective cover, but you need to put them together to make a book. You may need help to do this. You can staple, glue, tape, or sew with wool or string or even dental floss. Before you bind, be sure your cover and pages are in their correct numbered order.

Sharing

Share your book with your family, friends, younger children, seniors, classmates, teachers—whoever.

Each time you read your book aloud, you'll take pride in your ideas, the pleasure you're giving someone else, and your own hard work.

Something else will be happening inside you. Ideas will be stirring for a new book.

You've made it. You're an author and an illustrator!

Autograph, please!

The Way an Artist Speaks

Important Words

This is a review of the technical terms and the way they are used in the book.

ant's-eye view: the underview, as it might be seen by an ant.

background, midground, foreground: points of view.

binding: sewing, stapling, or taping your finished pages to make a book.

biography: information about you as the author/illustrator. This might be placed on page 1, or on the inside or outside of the book cover.

bird's-eye view: the overview, as it might be seen by a bird.

book mock-up: a page-by-page rough copy of your book, based on your storyboard. Characters have no detail. Words are not used, but can be printed and taped in.

camera angles: different points of view, such as horizontal, bird's-eye, ant's-eye, close-up. A variety of camera angles adds interest.

close-up: an enlargement of a specific part of a character or scene, such as a hand, eye, keyhole, or doorknob.

collage: a design or composition of various materials (colored paper, cloth, cutouts of magazine pictures, etc.) glued on a plain or patterned surface.

copyright notice: a small c enclosed in a circle, followed by your name as author/illustrator, and the year in which you completed the project.

copyright page: page 2, opposite the title page. This page includes the copyright notice and dedication.

cover: includes an image, the title in large letters, and the names of the author and illustrator.

composition: all the parts of your illustration (characters, setting, point of view, type) and how they fit together.

cropping: when part of the picture is cut off by the page or the border of the frame, similar to zooming in for a close-up.

cross-hatching: lines that cross over each other at different angles to create tones or shades.

double-page spread: a single picture or design spreading across facing pages

editing: correcting or changing items in your storyboard, book mock-up, or written story.

endpapers: the inside of the front and back covers, and sometimes their facing pages. These areas may be used for decorative purposes or left plain. The author's biography can be placed on the inside of the back cover.

frame or **panel:** one of the small squares on the storyboard or a comic page.

horizontal view: side-to-side; the horizon line and the characters and objects along it.

page turn: the suspenseful moment of turning the page, especially in a pattern book.

paste-up: pasting or gluing the typed or word-processed text onto the appropriate pages of your final book.

perspective: the way things are drawn to show depth or distance.

plot: see *storyline.*

pop-ups (plus *see-throughs, peepholes, pull-downs, foldouts*): techniques involving parts of the page that can be moved physically.

rough sketch: a quick sketch without detail that helps you think through and plan what you want in your picture.

spot illustration: a small illustration (a square, rectangle, or circle) placed on a page with text.

stick figures or **circle characters:** sketches that have little or no detail.

storyboard: a grid of small squares or frames for story planning. Words are not included, but short lines can be drawn to indicate where words will go later.

storyline or **plot:** what happens in your story.

text or **type:** the words in your book.

thumbnails: very small rough sketches, usually many on a page.

title page: page 3, usually the reverse side of the first page of your book. This page includes the title, without illustration, and the names of the author and illustrator.

turnaround: the climax or turning point in your story. This usually occurs around frames #11 to #15 of your storyboard.

vertical view: up and down.

wraparound: one-piece protective cover that wraps around a book. It includes both front and back covers.

Illustration Ideas

This glossary presents design ideas to help the author/illustrator discover interesting, unusual, and dynamic ways to illustrate a picture book, graphic novel, or comic strip. They are grouped under three headings: points of view, collage, and design.

Points of View

Horizontal

The horizontal (along the horizon) view is frequently used to make a normal, everyday picture, and suits a fairly calm or passive moment in a story. For more emotional or dramatic moments, other points of view should be considered.

Foreground, Midground, Background: Coming Toward You

The most important character should be placed up close, in the foreground, and made larger than the others. Thus, when this character is approaching, the facial expression is more likely to catch the viewer's attention.

Foreground, Midground, Background: Going Away

When characters face away from the viewer, the emotional intensity diminishes. This arrangement of foreground/midground/background creates an impression that the action is passing by.

Bird's-Eye View

The bird's-eye view is an overview that shows where the action is taking place. From above, the viewer sees everything that's going on but is, for the moment, safely removed from any danger in the action below. This point of view creates a sense of power.

Ant's-Eye View

The ant's-eye view can be likened to that of small children who, of physical necessity, must look up at much of their surroundings. Adults must seem like giants. This underview, then, tends to diminish the power of the viewer.

Close-Up: Full Face, Part of a Sequence

By focusing or concentrating the viewer's attention, the close-up often conveys intense emotion, especially if it is a double-page spread or full frame. It can be used frequently once the full features of the character have been established.

Close-Up: Full Face, Front View

The close-up, especially if it's a face, confronts the viewer. This is like having someone stand very close and then suddenly move into your personal space. All your senses become alert at once!

Close-Up: Four Designs

Whether on a single page or part of a double-page spread, the close-up gets the viewer involved. "What's the matter with this baby? Why is it crying so hard?"

Extreme Close-Up: Side View, Cropped

Extreme close-ups are frequently cropped. This means that the full picture would extend beyond the page or illustration border. These can be very dramatic, particularly if they are faces expressing intense emotion.

Extreme Close-Up: Background Details

An extreme close-up doesn't always have to be a face—it can be a finger pointing in a crucial direction, a hand turning a strange doorknob, or a raised foot on a sandy beach. In such cases, background details contribute to the overall impression.

Foreground: Six Views

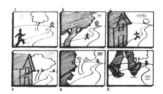

By rearranging three elements (person, house, and tree), the artist alters the composition to emphasize the important foreground subject. Since foreground objects are generally darker than background ones, they have been shaded.

Collage

Cutout: Face Details

Simple shapes, which are easy to cut out, can turn into a moustache, eyebrows, eyes, or a bow tie when glued to a basic head outline. This technique gives maximum design effect with minimum effort.

Cutout: Patterned Paper

Cutout pieces of patterned paper (wallpaper, gift wrap, or even patterned cloth) can be arranged to create a colorful and dramatic scene. A dark-colored background will enhance the design by making the various elements stand out.

Cutout: Interior Perspective

Interior designs have foreground, midground, and background areas, just as outdoor settings have. The proximity, however, makes the handling of interior perspective more difficult.

Cutout: Wavy Lines

A simple yet effective underwater scene can be created by cutting a large sheet of blue construction paper into wavy strips, separating them slightly, and mounting them on a light-colored background. Words in air bubbles (where else?) and elements of Neptune's world can be added as desired.

Cutout: Silhouette on Drawn Landscape

Black paper silhouette cutouts can be used to create dramatic foreground and background effects. Varying textures of grass, distant fields, buildings, and sky can be conveyed by a combination of lines, dots, and shapes.

Cutout: Positive and Negative Shapes

Unusual effects can be achieved by planning a collage so that both the cutout parts (the positive shapes) and the remaining open spaces (the negative shapes) are used.

Cutout: Parts Rearranged

One way to make an image more interesting or dynamic is to give it movement. The image is cut into horizontal (or vertical) strips, which are separated slightly, moved to the right or left (or up or down) and mounted on a lighter or contrasting background.

Cutout and Torn Shapes

Drawing and printing with white pencil crayon on black paper can produce some unusual images. These, combined with cutout and torn shapes, can be mounted on a light or contrasting background for spectacular results.

Cutout: Photo and Drawing Combined

A collage of carefully selected magazine pictures, cartoon cutouts, word balloons, and comic-strip lettering (newspaper headlines would do as well) is made to order for the person who exclaims, "But I can't draw!"

Design

Type Placement: Seven Positions

Words, also called type or text, are usually placed at the top of an illustrated page, but this is not a fixed rule. They can go anywhere, as long as a space has been left for them, but they should never be squeezed in as an afterthought.

Cover Designs: Four Examples

Designing the cover usually comes last (along with the title) in a book-making project. Whether a repetition of a picture from inside the book or a totally new illustration, the cover design should be regarded as a *grand finale*.

Lettering Styles

Since many words have their own visual characteristics, a lettering style can be selected or designed to give a word personality. The individual letters, however, must be legible, and the words recognizable.

Storyboard Templates

The storyboard project described in this book is based on a 24-page book (a total of 28 frames, including front and back covers, inside and outside). For young children or for other projects, the format can be modified to 12 pages (16 frames, including covers), 10 pages (14 frames, including covers), or even 6 pages (8 frames—three double-page spreads and outside covers only).

Storyboards for Graphic Novels and Comics

Here are some straightforward double-page layouts. See how easy it is to follow the sequence. Double-page spreads present both pages at the same time, so remember to think about the design as two pages viewed together.

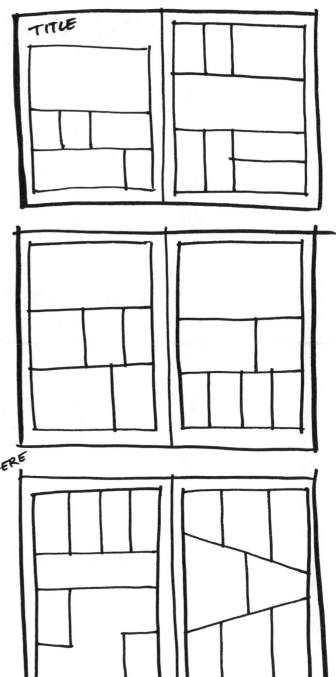

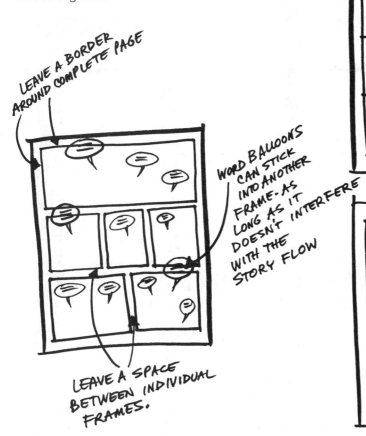

LEAVE A BORDER AROUND COMPLETE PAGE

WORD BALLOONS CAN STICK INTO ANOTHER FRAME. AS LONG AS IT DOESN'T INTERFERE WITH THE STORY FLOW

LEAVE A SPACE BETWEEN INDIVIDUAL FRAMES.

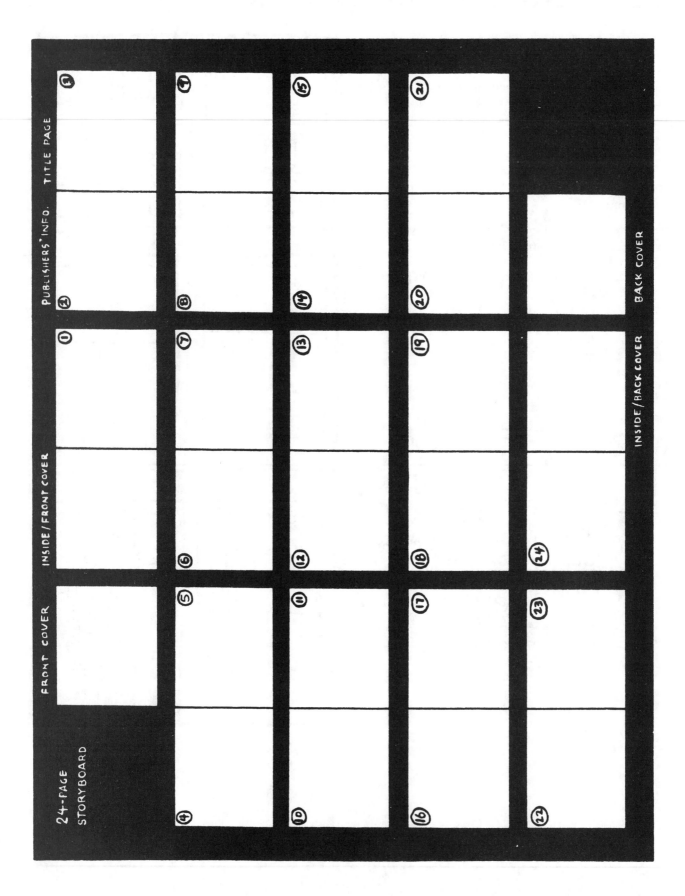

6-page Storyboard

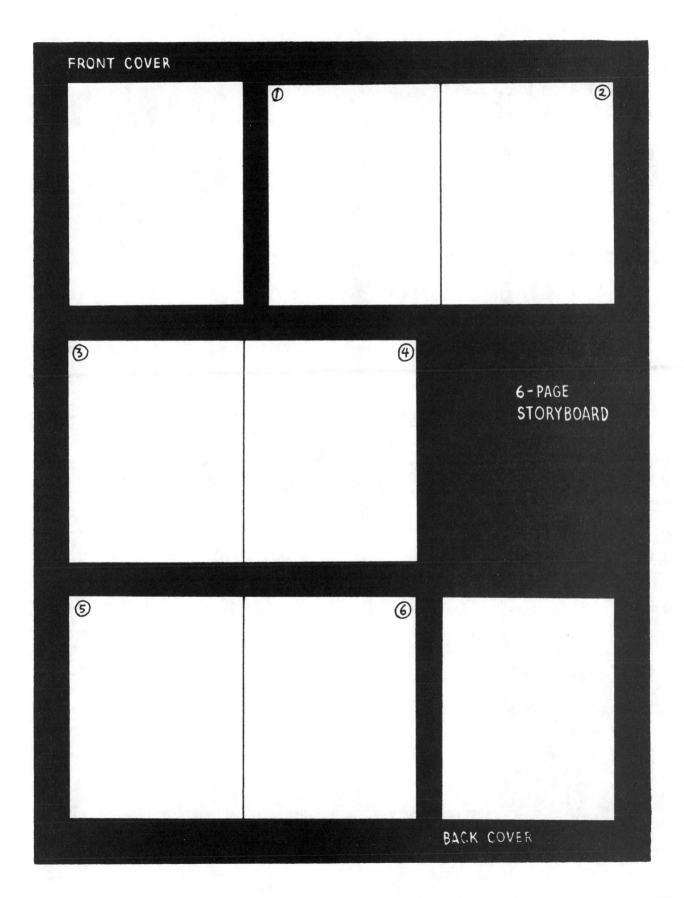

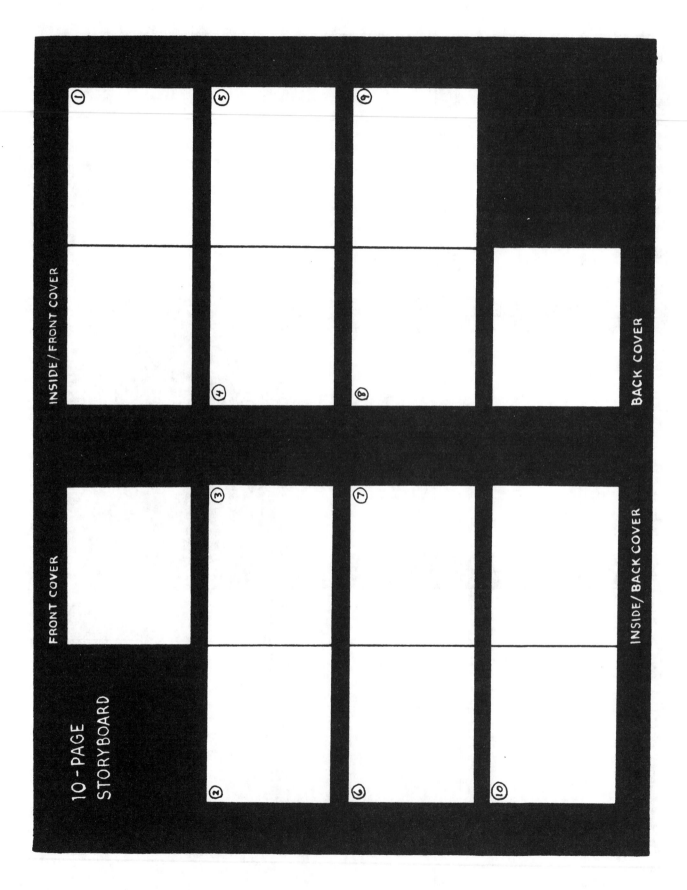

12-PAGE STORYBOARD

FRONT COVER

INSIDE/FRONT COVER

①

②

③

④

⑤

⑥

⑦

⑧

⑨

⑩

⑪

⑫

INSIDE/BACK COVER

BACK COVER

Index